Run, Oscar, Run!

Storybook ~~Walk~~ RUN Edition

How to:

1. Cut.
Open book. Place only the inside book pages in a paper cutter and cut on the dotted line. If necessary, tear or cut pages out of book first and then trim.

2) Laminate.
Place two pages together in a 11 x 17 laminate pouch. All spreads have page numbers for sorting on the back.

3) Display.
Place on Storybook Walk displays or use ideas below.

Instructions for walk:

This storybook walk can be set up either outside or in a gymnasium. Make sure the story is set up in a place where it is acceptable for children to run freely. You do not need to hang up this story in a straight line, only in chronological order. There is an activity prompt summary at the end of the story to help you set up your walk.

Outside:
If you are setting up your walk outside, you will need to have a tree close to page 2. If you have no trees use the example tree page from the end of the book. Why not set up the walk around the playground and see how many children read the book during a break?

Indoor:
This will require some creativity but should work well. You can either hang up the pages of the story along the walls of the gymnasium, on objects, or you can place them on the floor and have the children pick them up to read. It may be a good idea to mark Oscar's path to school with cones so that the children always follow the same path.

Published in 2024 by Kelley Donner at KelleyDonner.com
Text Copyright © 2024 Kelley Donner; Illustration Copyright © 2024 Kelley Donner

All rights reserved. No part of this book may be used in any manner without written permission of the copyright owner except for the use as a storybook walk.

First Edition 2024
ISBN 978-1-955698-18-4 Paperback
ISBN: 978-1-955698- 17-7 Storybook Walk Edition

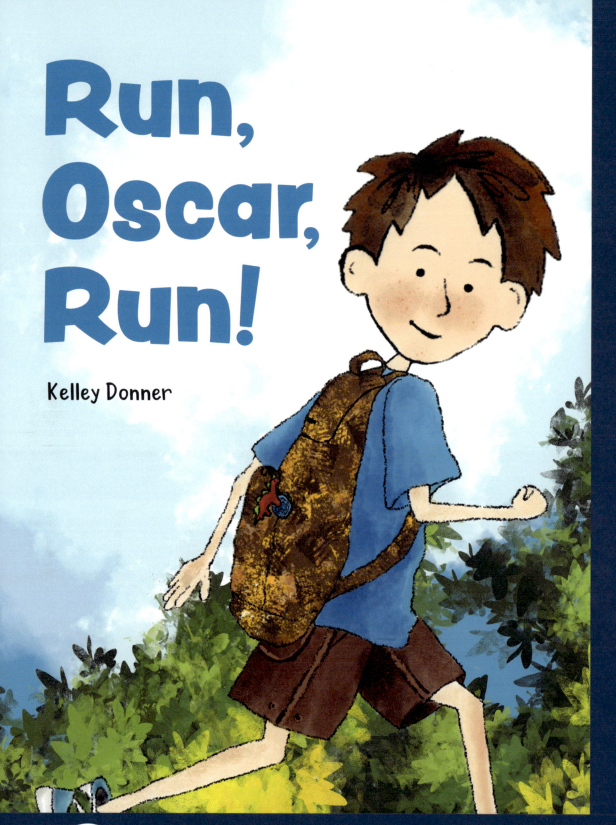

Run, Oscar, Run!

Kelley Donner

Run, Oscar, Run!

Copyright © KelleyDonner 2024

Start

Activity Prompt:

Are you ready to read and run? The story begins on the next page. Do some stretches and then proceed to page 2.

As Oscar walked past the old oak tree on his way to school one morning, he tripped and scraped his knee.

Oscar wondered why he fell, and he suddenly had a strange feeling in his tummy.

Run, Oscar, Run!

Copyright © KelleyDonner 2024

Activity Prompt:

Pretend you are walking to school with Oscar. Go back to the start.
Then walk around the tree and head to page 3.

So the next day, Oscar crossed the street so that he wouldn't pass the old oak

tree.

Run, Oscar, Run!

Copyright © KelleyDonner 2024

As he continued walking down the old sidewalk which was damaged and full of cracks, a car stopped at a nearby house.

It honked its horn loudly.

Oscar cringed, covered his ears, and thought to himself...

I hate loud noises! It must be those **cracks!**

I bet, I stepped on one and it caused me to have bad luck!

Activity Prompt:
Go back to the start. Walk around the tree.
Then tiptoe to page 4. Imagine you are avoiding the cracks in the sidewalk.

So the next day,
Oscar crossed the street so
that he wouldn't pass the old oak **tree.**

And, then he tip-toed down
the broken sidewalk being ever so
careful not to step on any **cracks.**

No car honked its horn
and Oscar continued
on his way to school.

At the next corner,
a butterfly flew
out of a bush.

Run, Oscar, Run!

Copyright © KelleyDonner 2024

Oscar watched the butterfly as it danced through the air unaware of anything or anyone around it.

Not looking where he was going, he stepped in a puddle. Oscar felt the water creep into his shoes.

He sighed and thought,

That silly **butterfly!** It made me step in that puddle. I should have known it was out to get me, too.

Activity Prompt:

Go back to the start. Run around the tree. Tiptoe past page 3. Then turn four circles like you are a butterfly and head to page 5.

So the next day,
Oscar crossed the street so
that he wouldn't pass the old oak **tree.**

Then he carefully tiptoed
down the damaged sidewalk
making sure not to step on any **cracks.**

He made sure not to look toward the bush.

A **butterfly**

didn't fly out in front of him and
he didn't step in a puddle.

Satifsfied that everything was okay,
he continued on his way...

Run, Oscar, Run!

Copyright © KelleyDonner 2024

But then, rain began to fall making him uncomfortably wet. His mom had told him that it would be sunny today.

Oscar wondered if he had somehow caused the rain and his tummy hurt again.

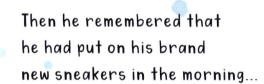

Then he remembered that he had put on his brand new sneakers in the morning...

Oscar thought...

It must be my new **sneakers!** They have caused the rain! Tomorrow, I will wear my old shoes.

Activity Prompt:

Go back to the start. Run around the tree. Tiptoe past page 3. Turn four circles past page 4. Touch your toes at page 5. Then run to page 6.

As he opened the door, Oscar suddenly had a horrible feeling in his tummy.

He looked down the sidewalk and thought about

the old oak **tree**,

the sidewalk full of **cracks**,

and the bush with many **butterflies**...

Activity Prompt:

Try to stand still for 30 seconds straight! Then go to page 7.

He remembered all of the bad things
that had happened to him that week.
He did not want to risk that he might

scrape his knee,
hear loud noises,
step in a puddle,
or get soaked in the rain again,

But...
he couldn't imagine
being late for school.

Oscar was never late for school!

Activity Prompt:

Breathe in deep. Hold for 10 seconds. Then exhale.
Do 10 jumping jacks and run to page 8.

Oscar ran past the old oak **tree** where he had fallen and hurt his knee...

but, he did not trip and fall.

Oscar thought to himself...

I'm okay.

Nothing happened.

Activity Prompt:
Go back to the start. Count to 3 and then run as fast as you can to page 9.

Then Oscar ran over the broken sidewalk, wincing everytime he stepped on a crack...

but, nothing happened.
There were no loud noises.

Run, Oscar, Run!

Activity Prompt:
Go back to the start. Now run all the way to page 10 even faster than you ran before.

Oscar ran past the bush with the **butterflies.**

Suddenly, a butterfly flew directly in front of him.

Oscar stopped abruptly and looked at the butterfly twist and turn through the sky,

but, he did not step in the puddle.

Run, Oscar, Run!

Copyright © KelleyDonner 2024

"I'm okay."

thought Oscar, finally believing the words this time.

He continued to repeat them in his head with every step...

"I'm okay. I'm okay. I'm okay!"

Activity Prompt:

Pretend you are a butterfly. Fly around the tree and then continue on to page 11.

As Oscar ran further, he began to think:

Run, Oscar, Run!

Copyright © KelleyDonner 2024

Perhaps the oak **tree** did not cause me to fall.

And, the **cracks** did not cause the loud noises.

And, the **butterfly** did not make me step in a puddle.

Maybe... my **new shoes**...

...did not actually cause the rain!

Activity Prompt:

Are you happy for Oscar? Jump up as high as you can. Then go to page 12.

The next day, Oscar got ready for school and put on his brand **new shoes.**

Run, Oscar, Run!

Copyright © KelleyDonner 2024

"I'm going to be okay!"

he thought, as he skipped past the old oak tree.

And...

Activity Prompt:
Go back to the start. Then skip all the way to the page 13.

Run, Oscar, Run!

Copyright © KelleyDonner 2024

...nothing
bad happened.

Oscar made it to school
in record time.

He looked back down the path.
Then he looked ahead and smiled.

Today was going to be a great day.

(The End)

Activity Prompt:

You did it! You helped Oscar make it to school. That was a lot of running! Pat yourself on the back and shout, "I did it!"

Would you like to read and run?

1. Go to page 1.

2. Read the story on each page.

3. Follow the activity prompts on the bottom of each page.

4. When you are finished, go to your teacher and get a sticker.

5. Have fun!

Would you like to get children reading during recess and after school? Why not hang up Run, Oscar, Run! on the playground and let children read it for fun? You can laminate and hang up the sheet above so that children can figure out how to do everything by themselves.

Run, Oscar, Run! - Copyright © KelleyDonner 2023

Tree

Do you need a tree for your storybook walk? Then cut out this tree, laminate it, and use it instead. Tape it to a wall or hang it on a fence and have children tap it instead of running around it. Tape it to a cone, stake, or coloumn. Be creative and have fun.

Run, Oscar, Run! - Copyright © KelleyDonner 2023

Activity Prompt Summary

● (Each dot below represents one page in the story):

Page 1. This is just the beginning. This book requires a lot of action. Are you ready? **Do some stretches** and then head to page 2.

Page 2: Pretend you are walking to school with Oscar. **Go back to the start.** Then **walk around the tree** and **head to page 3**.

Page 3. **Go back to the start. Walk around the tree**. Then **tip toe to page 4**. Imagine you are avoiding the cracks in the sidewalk.

Page 4: **Go back to the start. Run around the tree. Tip-toe past page 3.** Then **turn four circles** like you are a butterfly and head to page 5.

Page 5: **Go back to the start. Run around the tree. Tip-toe past page 3. Turn four circles past page 4. Touch your toes at page 5.** Then **run to page 6**.

Page 6: Try to **stand still for 30 seconds** straight!

Page 7: **Breathe in deep. Hold for 10 seconds**, then exhale. **Do 10 jumping jacks** and **run to page 8.**

Page 8: **Go back to the start. Count to 3** and **then run as fast as you can to page 9**.

Page 9: **Go back to the start.** Now run all the way to page 10 even faster than you ran before.

Page 10: Pretend you are a butterfly. **Fly around the tree** and then **continue on to page 11**.

Page 11: Are you happy for Oscar? **Jump up and shout, "Hooray!"**

Page 12: **Go back to the start.** Then **skip all the way to the page 13.**

Page 13: You did it! You helped Oscar make it to school. **Pat yourself on the back and shout, "I did it!"**

Run, Oscar, Run! - Copyright © KelleyDonner 2024

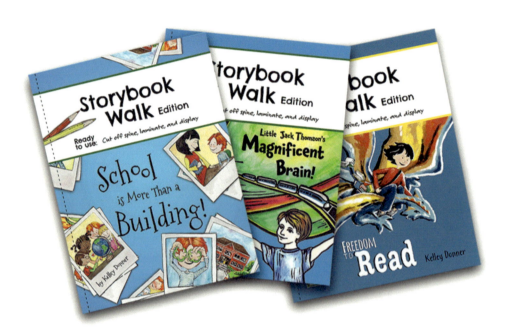

For more storybook walk ideas, head to

StorybookWalk.com

Made in the USA
Columbia, SC
19 June 2025

59562334R00035